I0737516

ASSESSMENT OF Story Comprehension

ASC™

ADMINISTRATION AND SCORING FORMS

Child's Name ______________________________

Sex ______________________________

Date of Birth ______________________________

Summary of ASC Administrations and Scores						
	Form 1	Form 2	Form 3	Form 4	Form 5	Form 6
Date						
Examiner						
Score						

Manufactured in the U.S.A.
PACKAGE — DO NOT BREAK.

ISBN-13: 978-1-68125-236-0
ISBN-10: 1-68125-236-8
90000
9 781681 252360

Trina D. Spencer, Ph.D., BCBA-D
Howard Goldstein, Ph.D., CCC-SLP

Assessment of Story Comprehension ASC™

1 Carlos and the Big Hill

Child's name ____________________

Examiner ____________________

Date ____________________

You are going to listen to a story. It is called *Carlos and the Big Hill.*

Hmm. I wonder what will happen in this story. Let's think about the title, *Carlos and the Big Hill.* What do you think will happen?

1.		0 1 2

Now you are going to listen to the story. Listen carefully because I am going to ask you some questions about the story. Are you ready?

A few days ago, Carlos was riding his new black bike on the sidewalk. He rode up and down the sidewalk in front of his house.

When Carlos rode past his neighbor's house, he started going down a big hill. Then Carlos' bike hit a bump in the sidewalk. He fell off his bike and injured his arm. Carlos cut his arm on the rough ground.

Carlos was sad.

He picked up his bike and slowly walked home. He found his mom and said, "Mommy, I fell and injured myself. My arm is cut."

His mom gently cleaned his cut. Then she put a bandage on his arm. After Carlos got a bandage, his mom gave him a hug. He asked his mom if she would watch him ride his new bike. She said, "Of course. I want to watch you, but don't injure yourself again." Carlos rode his bike so well that his mom clapped and cheered for him.

Thanks for listening. Now I am going to ask you some questions.

ASC™ 1. Carlos and the Big Hill *(continued)*

2.	**What was Carlos doing in this story?**		0 1 2
3.	**In this story, Carlos was sad. Why was Carlos sad?**		0 1 2
4.	**Carlos fell off his bike and cut his arm. What happened next?**		0 1 2
5.	**Why do you think Carlos's mom gave him a hug?**		0 1 2
6.	**What happened at the end of the story?**		0 1 2
7.	**The next time Carlos rides his bike, do you think he will go down a big hill? Why/why not?** If child does not tell why, then use the prompt: ❐ **Okay, now tell me why.**		0 1 2
8a.	**What does *injure* mean?**		0 2 3
If child does not say "to hurt something" or "to get hurt," then ask:			
8b.	**Does *injure* mean to cook something or <u>to hurt something</u>?** (Circle response)		0 1
*** If child responds with the word *because* for Items 3, 5, and 7, then use the prompt, "Because why?"**			
		Total score	17

Child's performance was a valid representation of his or her ability.

❐ Yes ❐ No

Examiner notes: ____________________

Assessment of Story Comprehension ASC™

2 Lina and Her Noisy Friend

Child's name ______________________

Examiner ______________________

Date ______________________

You are going to listen to a story. It is called *Lina and Her Noisy Friend.*

Hmm. I wonder what will happen in this story. Let's think about the title, *Lina and Her Noisy Friend.* What do you think will happen?

1.		0 1 2

Now you are going to listen to the story. Listen carefully because I am going to ask you some questions about the story. Are you ready?

Yesterday at naptime Lina was resting under a soft, warm blanket. The classroom was silent. No one made any noise. Lina closed her eyes and quickly fell asleep.

Lina's friend Michelle lay on a mat next to her. Michelle was looking around the room and pulled on Lina's soft blanket. When Michelle said Lina's name, it woke her up. Lina whispered quietly, "Shhh. I am trying to sleep!" Michelle said, "I'm not tired. I want to talk." Lina knew they should be silent during naptime. They should be quiet, but Michelle kept talking.

Lina was mad.

Then Lina raised her hand. She asked nicely if she could move her mat. Her teacher said it was okay. Lina carried her mat to a dark corner on the other side of the room.

After Lina moved her mat, it was silent again. It was so quiet that she fell asleep right away. Then Lina had nice dreams until naptime was over.

Thanks for listening. Now I am going to ask you some questions.

ASC™ 2. Lina and Her Noisy Friend *(continued)*

2.	**What was Lina doing in this story?**		0 1 2
3.	**In this story, Lina was mad. Why was Lina mad?**		0 1 2
4.	**Lina's friend Michelle kept talking to her during naptime. What happened next?**		0 1 2
5.	**Why do you think Lina did not want to talk to Michelle?**		0 1 2
6.	**What happened at the end of the story?**		0 1 2
7.	**Do you think Lina will put her mat next to Michelle at the next naptime? Why/why not?** If child does not tell why, then use the prompt: ❒ ***Okay, now tell me* why.**		0 1 2
8a.	**What does *silent* mean?**		0 2 3
If child does not say "quiet," then ask:			
8b.	**Does *silent* mean quiet or hot?** (Circle response)		0 1
***If child responds with the word *because* for Items 3, 5, and 7, then use the prompt, "Because why?"**			
		Total score	17

Child's performance was a valid representation of his or her ability.

❒ Yes ❒ No

Examiner notes: ____________________

____

____

____

____

Assessment of Story Comprehension ASC™

3 Hannah and Her Favorite Toy

Child's name ______________________

Examiner ______________________

Date ______________________

You are going to listen to a story. It is called *Hannah and Her Favorite Toy.*

Hmm. I wonder what will happen in this story. Let's think about the title, *Hannah and Her Favorite Toy.* What do you think will happen?

1.		0 1 2

Now you are going to listen to the story. Listen carefully because I am going to ask you some questions about the story. Are you ready?

Yesterday Hannah was in her room packing her backpack. She packed her folders, pencils, and crayons. She was also going to take her favorite toy airplane to show to her class. She took the plane out of her toy box and gently put it in her backpack.

Then Hannah remembered a book that she forgot to pack. When she put the book in her backpack, she heard a loud crunch. She quickly took the airplane out of her bag, but it was damaged. The wing of the plane was broken.

Hannah was sad.

Then Hannah found her dad. She said, "My airplane is damaged. It is broken." Hannah's dad said, "Don't worry. Here is some glue to fix your broken toy." Hannah carefully glued the thin wing back onto her plane.

After she glued the wing back on, Hannah's toy was not damaged. It was like new. Hannah set her airplane on her shelf to let the glue dry.

Thanks for listening. Now I am going to ask you some questions.

ASC™ 3. Hannah and Her Favorite Toy *(continued)*

2.	**What was Hannah doing in this story?**		0 1 2
3.	**In this story, Hannah was sad. Why was Hannah sad?**		0 1 2
4.	**Hannah's favorite toy broke. What happened next?**		0 1 2
5.	**Why do you think Hannah's dad helped her fix her toy?**		0 1 2
6.	**What happened at the end of the story?**		0 1 2
7.	**Do you think Hannah will still take her toy plane to school? Why/why not?** If child does not tell why, then use the prompt: ❐ ***Okay, now tell me* why.**		0 1 2
8a.	**What does *damaged* mean?**		0 2 3
If child does not say "broken," then ask:			
8b.	**Does *damaged* mean broken or colorful?** (Circle response)		0 1
***If child responds with the word *because* for Items 3, 5, and 7, then use the prompt, "Because why?"**			
	Total score		17

Child's performance was a valid representation of his or her ability.

❐ Yes ❐ No

Examiner notes: ______________________________

____

____

____

____

Assessment of Story Comprehension (ASC™), by Trina D. Spencer and Howard Goldstein.

Assessment of Story Comprehension ASC™

4 Jamal and the Nice Picture

Child's name ____________________

Examiner ____________________

Date ____________________

You are going to listen to a story. It is called *Jamal and the Nice Picture.*

Hmm. I wonder what will happen in this story. Let's think about the title, *Jamal and the Nice Picture.* What do you think will happen?

1.		0 1 2

Now you are going to listen to the story. Listen carefully because I am going to ask you some questions about the story. Are you ready?

Last week at school, Jamal and Angie were painting at a little table. Jamal was painting a huge fire truck. Angie was painting a bird.

Jamal's painting was almost done. It just needed a little red paint. When Jamal put his brush in the paint cup, it fell over. Red paint spilled all over Angie's painting. "Oh no! I messed up your bird," Jamal said.

Jamal was very sad.

Angie's painting was a mess, but Jamal did not know what to do. He slowly put his head down on the table. After thinking about what he should do, Jamal apologized to Angie. Jamal said, "I'm sorry for spilling on your painting." Then he gave Angie the picture that he painted.

Angie said, "Thanks. I like fire trucks, too." Apologizing was the right thing to do. Saying sorry to Angie helped her feel better. Then Jamal and Angie worked together to paint another bird. They had fun painting with each other.

Thanks for listening. Now I am going to ask you some questions.

ASC 4. Jamal and the Nice Picture *(continued)*

2.	**What was Jamal doing in this story?**		0 1 2
3.	**In this story, Jamal was sad. Why was Jamal sad?**		0 1 2
4.	**Jamal spilled paint on Angie's painting. What happened next?**		0 1 2
5.	**Why do you think Jamal gave Angie his fire truck painting?**		0 1 2
6.	**What happened at the end of the story?**		0 1 2
7.	**Do you think Angie will paint with Jamal again? Why/why not?** If child does not tell why, then use the prompt: ❐ ***Okay, now tell me* why.**		0 1 2
8a.	**What does *apologize* mean?**		0 2 3
If child does not say "to say sorry" or "say sorry," then ask:			
8b.	**Does *apologize* mean to ask a question or to say sorry?** (Circle response)		0 1
***If child responds with the word *because* for Items 3, 5, and 7, then use the prompt, "Because why?"**			
		Total score	17

Child's performance was a valid representation of his or her ability.

❐ Yes ❐ No

Examiner notes: ______________________________

____

____

____

____

Assessment of Story Comprehension ASC™

5 Tony and His Messy Things

Child's name ______________________

Examiner ______________________

Date ______________________

You are going to listen to a story. It is called *Tony and His Messy Things.*

Hmm. I wonder what will happen in this story. Let's think about the title, *Tony and His Messy Things.* What do you think will happen?

1.		0 1 2

Now you are going to listen to the story. Listen carefully because I am going to ask you some questions about the story. Are you ready?

Last weekend, Tony asked if his friend Mikey could come over to play in his bedroom. Tony had a new racetrack to show him.

His mom said, "You will have to clean your room first. It needs to be tidy." His toys, books, and clothes were all over his bedroom floor, but he didn't want to pick them up.

Tony was mad.

Then Tony suddenly thought, "It *is* more fun to play in a tidy room." He quickly started to pick up toys, books, and clothes off his floor and put them away. Cleaning his room wasn't so bad.

After Tony cleaned his room, he looked around. His room was very tidy. His things were not all over the floor. Then there was more open space to play. There was even space to lay out the giant toy racetrack that he wanted to show Mikey. When Mikey came over, they had fun playing with the racetrack in Tony's clean room.

Thanks for listening. Now I am going to ask you some questions.

ASC™ 5. Tony and His Messy Things *(continued)*

2.	**Where did Tony want to play?**		0 1 2
3.	**In this story, Tony was mad. Why was Tony mad?**		0 1 2
4.	**Tony's mom told him to put away his things. What happened next?**		0 1 2
5.	**Why do you think Tony's mom told him to clean his room first?**		0 1 2
6.	**What happened at the end of the story?**		0 1 2
7.	**Do you think Tony will put his things away the next time his mom asks him to? Why/why not?** If child does not tell why, then use the prompt: ❐ ***Okay, now tell me* why.**		0 1 2
8a.	**What does *tidy* mean?**		0 2 3
If child does not say "clean," then ask:			
8b.	**Does *tidy* mean <u>clean</u> or heavy?** (Circle response)		0 1
*If child responds with the word *because* for Items 3, 5, and 7, then use the prompt, "Because why?"			
	Total score		17

Child's performance was a valid representation of his or her ability.

❐ Yes ❐ No

Examiner notes: ____________________

Assessment of Story Comprehension ASC™

6 Rosa and the Shiny Slide

Child's name ______________________

Examiner ______________________

Date ______________________

You are going to listen to a story. It is called *Rosa and the Shiny Slide.*

Hmm. I wonder what will happen in this story. Let's think about the title, *Rosa and the Shiny Slide.* What do you think will happen?

1.		0 1 2

Now you are going to listen to the story. Listen carefully because I am going to ask you some questions about the story. Are you ready?

One warm day, Rosa walked to the playground with her friend Shane. There was a shiny new slide that they wanted to play on.

When Shane and Rosa got to the playground, Rosa quickly ran to the slide. She climbed up the ladder and sat at the top. Shane climbed up behind her. Then Rosa asked Shane to give her a little push, but he shoved her really hard. She flew to the bottom of the slide and banged her knees on the ground.

Rosa was mad.

After Shane slid down the slide, Rosa told him, "It is not nice to shove! I asked you to give me a little push." Then Rosa asked Shane to help her climb to the top of the slide again.

Shane said, "I did not mean to shove you so hard." This time he gave Rosa a gentle push. The two friends played together on the slide for the rest of the day.

Thanks for listening. Now I am going to ask you some questions.

ASC™ 6. Rosa and the Shiny Slide *(continued)*

2.	**Where did Rosa and her friend Shane go in this story?**		0 1 2
3.	**In this story, Rosa was mad. Why was Rosa mad?**		0 1 2
4.	**Rosa banged her knees on the ground. What happened next?**		0 1 2
5.	**Why do you think Rosa told Shane not to shove?**		0 1 2
6.	**What happened at the end of the story?**		0 1 2
7.	**Do you think Rosa and Shane will play together again? Why/why not?** If child does not tell why, then use the prompt: ❒ ***Okay, now tell me* why.**		0 1 2
8a.	**What does *shove* mean?**		0 2 3
If child does not say "to push" or "push," then ask:			
8b.	**Does *shove* mean to push or to run?** (Circle response)		0 1
***If child responds with the word *because* for Items 3, 5, and 7, then use the prompt, "Because why?"**			
		Total score	17

Child's performance was a valid representation of his or her ability.

❒ Yes ❒ No

Examiner notes: ____________________

____

____

____

____

PAGE INTENTIONALLY LEFT BLANK.

PAGE INTENTIONALLY LEFT BLANK.

·P A U L·H·
BROOKES
PUBLISHING CO®

Typeset by Progressive Publishing Services, York, Pennsylvania.

Manufactured in the United States of America by H&N Printing & Graphics, Inc., Timonium, Maryland.

To contact the publisher:
Paul H. Brookes Publishing Co.
Post Office Box 10624
Baltimore, Maryland 21285-0624
1-800-638-3775; 1-410-337-9580
Fax: 1-410-337-8539
www.brookespublishing.com

The Assessment of Story Comprehension (ASC™) is intended for one-time use only and can be purchased in packages of 10.

For information on bulk sales, contact Paul H. Brookes Publishing Co.'s Sales Manager
at sales@brookespublishing.com or call one of the numbers listed above.